Precarious Lives

Jean Watkins was born in West Yorkshire and has lived near Reading for many years. She taught children with specific learning difficulties before gaining a BA in English from Reading University in 2001. Her poems have been widely published in magazines and anthologies. She has read regularly at the town's Poets' Café and at various venues further afield.

Other books by the same author

Scrimshaw (Two Rivers Press, 2013)

Also by Two Rivers poets

David Attwooll, *The Sound Ladder* (2015)
Kate Behrens, *The Beholder* (2012)
Kate Behrens, *Man with Bombe Alaska* (2016)
Adrian Blamires, *The Pang Valley* (2010)
Adrian Blamires & Peter Robinson (eds.), *The Arts of Peace* (2014)
David Cooke, *A Murmuration* (2015)
Terry Cree, *Fruit* (2014)
Claire Dyer, *Eleven Rooms* (2013)
Claire Dyer, *Interference Effects* (2016)
John Froy, *Sandpaper & Seahorses* (2018)
A. F. Harrold, *The Point of Inconvenience* (2013)
Ian House, *Nothing's Lost* (2014)
Gill Learner, *The Agister's Experiment* (2011)
Gill Learner, *Chill Factor* (2016)
Sue Leigh, *Chosen Hill* (2018)
Becci Louise, *Octopus Medicine* (2017)
Mairi MacInnes, *Amazing Memories of Childhood, etc.* (2016)
Steven Matthews, *On Magnetism* (2017)
Henri Michaux, *Storms under the Skin* translated by Jane Draycott (2017)
Tom Phillips, *Recreation Ground* (2012)
John Pilling & Peter Robinson (eds.), *The Rilke of Ruth Speirs:*
    New Poems, Duino Elegies, Sonnets to Orpheus & Others (2015)
Peter Robinson, *English Nettles and Other Poems* (2010)
Peter Robinson (ed.), *Reading Poetry: An Anthology* (2011)
Peter Robinson (ed.), *A Mutual Friend: Poems for Charles Dickens* (2012)
Peter Robinson, *Foreigners, Drunks and Babies: Eleven Stories* (2013)
Lesley Saunders, *Cloud Camera* (2012)
Lesley Saunders, *Nominy-Dominy* (2018)
Robert Seatter, *The Book of Snow* (2016)
Jack Thacker, *Handling* (2018)
Susan Utting, *Fair's Fair* (2012)
Susan Utting, *Half the Human Race* (2017)

Precarious Lives

Jean Watkins

First published in the UK in 2018 by Two Rivers Press
7 Denmark Road, Reading RG1 5PA
www.tworiverspress.com

© Jean Watkins 2018

The right of the poet to be identified as the author of this work has been asserted by her in accordance with the Copyright, Designs and Patents Act of 1988.

All rights reserved. No part of this publication may be reproduced, stored in or introduced into a retrieval system, or transmitted, in any form, or by any means (electronic, mechanical, photocopying, recording or otherwise) without the prior written permission of the publisher.

ISBN 978-1-909747-41-8

1 2 3 4 5 6 7 8 9

Two Rivers Press is represented in the UK by Inpress Ltd and distributed by NBNi.

Cover design and illustrations by Sally Castle
Text design by Nadja Guggi and typeset in Janson and Parisine

Printed and bound in Great Britain by Imprint Digital, Exeter

Acknowledgements

My thanks to the editors of the following journals, anthologies and website where some of the poems have appeared: *Acumen, Artemis Poetry, South*; *Running Before the Wind, Transitions, Songs for the Unsung* (all Grey Hen Press); *Reading Creative Arts Anthology*; *Stanley Spencer Poems: An Anthology* (Two Rivers Press); *Ver Competition Anthology 2018* (thehighwindowpress.com).

I would also like to thank members of Reading's Thursday Group for their helpful comments on my poems; Peter Robinson, Adrian Blamires, Ian House and Two Rivers Press for their support.

Contents

Brute | 1
Marvel | 2
Trout | 3
Sandy Haven | 4
Regatta | 5
Fishwives | 6
The Village of Living Waters | 7
Turvey Remains Optimistic | 8
December Beechwood | 9
Suffolk Skies | 10
Dusk | 11
The Ruined House | 12
The Somerset House Conference 1604 | 13
Corsica II, about 1959 | 14
Czech Conscript | 15
San Gimignano | 16
In Tuscany | 17
Car Park | 18
At Pembroke Castle | 19
Rackham | 20
The Thing | 21
Our Gang | 22
Speech Training | 23
Severing | 24
Warming | 25
The Dragon Lands | 26
Fading | 27
Ever After | 28
Meeting her Eyes | 29
Papier Blanc | 30
OS Sheet 189: Land's End | 31
Pulse | 32
From the Kitchen Sink | 33
Wasps | 34
Thread | 35

Gown | 36
Master Glover | 37
Barbers' Bowl | 38
The Potato Eaters | 39
Disciples | 40
Hilda, Unity and Dolls | 41
Loch Alsh | 42
Greater Spotted | 43
Ghostly | 44
Mine | 45
Our Dream | 46
After Sonnet 64, Shakespeare | 47
Swift | 48

Brute

They took us to the edge of the world
where chaos heaved – a huge grey beast
slavering at the sand, sucking at stones.

Aged three I knew, refused to tempt it
though my sister ran shrieking in and out
shocked by the cold, thrilled at her daring.

I can taste the salt of my father's broken promise
when he let me go, water closed its lid,
in a green element I knew electric panic.

Now we herd between flags, minded by lifeguards
mindful of its malevolence; the airbed drifting
quietly to deep water, the pincers of an undertow.

I have heard its roar, seen fathoms flung on rocks
at Hell's Mouth, Bryher, exploding in white and silver,
read of the wrecks littering the Scillies' seaways.

A TV reporter on a beach points out the cliff
where a freak wave snatched two boys, or the spot
where a man trying to save his dog was drowned.

Marvel

because she is huge as an ocean liner,
airship, submerged continent. Because
she hugs the coast, her progress regal,

calf sheltered underneath. Because
she heads north, the annual rhythm
of to and fro grafted to her genes.

Because of the effrontery of her spouts,
richness of her milk, resounding thump
when her tail-flukes slap the surface.

Because in her world of filtered light
her low-pitched song sounds distances
to seek her kin, her kind, *blåhval*.

blåval is Norwegian for blue whale

Trout

After the woodcut by Allen Seaby, 1920

Pale tongue of mud or smudge of sand
below kingcups and a reaching shrub,

it hugs the bank, hidden, stippled skin
merging with ripples, sun-flecks.

Life-water pulses through the gills,
fins fan pearl space shading to blue,

fear tenses gut, glissades the spine,
a deep, unsleeping cell-echo of shock.

Sandy Haven

The path was edged with pebbles, shells stuck up from the wall
and over the road evening primroses grew on the dunes.
Not seen at home, the snails amazed – large greys
or brown and white coiled humbugs. They'd be
parked in shady corners, stuck under fuchsia leaves,
pulled off by my little sister and raced by my brother.

Back from the beach one day we saw a snail
half hidden in foam and swarmed over by ants;
a black attacking army. Dad said the foam was nasty,
would drive them off, but after tea I went to look again.
The ants and soft snail flesh had gone. The shell
was clean and empty as the seashells in my pail.

Regatta

you have to imagine the wind
a cold spray slap in the face
waves level   above you
salt smell   canvas creak
clinking of rigging on mast

prow slicing green water
you feel your blood race
the tilting   the tension
leaning out into space
to right her   about her

duck from the boom
as it swings   while
watching your footing
on heaving wet decks
and gripping the ropes

with blisters that burn
clouds join in the chase
as with fat straining sail
you shoot the home straight
set the final buoy rocking

Fishwives

Knives and talk flashing
gulls screaming,
we tighten shawls
against east wind
but still it cuts
into our red raw hands.

Our fingers slip
the guts into a bucket
or fling them to the gulls.
The smell never leaves us,
silver scales cover our pinnies.

We give the men some lip –
Sally tries the come-on.
We all watch out
for her, half-crazy
since her man was drowned.

I sense tide turn
before it slaps the jetty
watch men furling sails
as the *Mary Jane* comes into
harbour, cloud of gulls behind.
My Tom glides her into her berth.

The Village of Living Waters

I kneel to the stream running through my kabata
to wash crockery or clean vegetables. Carp
loom up to take morsels with delicate lips,

leaving the channel untainted. It's one of many
we split from the mountains' tumble, joined
again to flow to our paddy fields, tiered

down the valley. At dusk on special days
human souls flicker green above the rice tufts.
Disguised as fireflies, they are drawn to pure water.

Turvey Remains Optimistic*

that the Hainan gibbon – down to 25 individuals –
will be saved. An international team will employ
both forest corridors and artificial canopy bridges
to connect their fragmented habitat in the rainforests
of Hainan Island, China.

'They can disperse across a wider area;
there will be room for more social groups
to form and the population to grow,' said Turvey.

*Found poem

December Beechwood

I think of that silence
the pearl grey light
drizzle on my face

softness underfoot
my tread deadened
by mud and leaf mould

craning my neck to see
the tops of smooth grey trunks
high intertwining branches

mosses at their elephant feet
smooth or branching
like a mini coral reef

brambles with wizened berries
rain-bright jade and orange lichen
a robin's twitter out of sight

sweet smell of decay
tree fungi like wet plates
the stop-start dash of a squirrel
invisible when it freezes

Suffolk Skies

Cumulus

                        I was so
                accustomed to hills
        I expected to dislike East Anglia
but found its heights are in the sky.
I'd seen such clouds painted by Constable
but these were living, breathing, moving and growing
with slow dignity – like cruising swans, wings curved.

Cirrus

high up on clear blue days these wispy lines
are Grandma's hairs pulled from her comb

Nimbus

enter	black	conceal	tease
the	clouds	the	with
villain	driven	sun	drops
darkening	by	roof-in	then
our	wild	the	drench
day	westerlies	town	us

Cirrocumulus

    (a) (mackerel) (sky) (seems) (so) (benign)
    (an) (aerial) (spread) (of) (silver) (scales)
    (but) (do) (not) (let) (its) (symmetry) (deceive)
    (it) (is) (the) (mail-clad) (herald) (of) (a) (storm)

Dusk

After *Grey and Silver*: Whistler

Border of day and night, land
and river, high and low tide.

Green-grey, a dull sheen
on the water, moored boats
smudges, a furled sail doubled.

Dark factories. Tall chimneys
still gush smoke to mist
a spire then alchemize
to silver with the clouds.

Now rats slip through the slime
the incoming tide slaps steps
and rocks the sleeping craft.

Smells of salt and mud
a gull's diminishing cry.

The Ruined House
John Sell Cotman: c. 1807–10

What made him choose this half-abandoned house –
it leans, walls sag, the gable held together by a board.
End wall collapsed, supported by the timber frame,
it stands wide open to the weather and our gaze.

How tenderly he has shaped each brick
where the wall fell away, each slat
in the rough fence round the upper floor,
dark shapes behind, a coiled rope on a hook.

This wooden staircase must have resounded
to many fathers' boots and children's clatter.
The bedroom could never contain childbirth screams,
or boards exclude the smell of boiling cabbage.

Against grey sky the artist shows weak sun lighting
gable and lime-washed cob. In spite of gravel heaped
downstairs, the house has dignity, the way it thrusts
its narrow height against the sky, defiant in old age.

The Somerset House Conference 1604
Artist unknown

You are arrested by their gaze. Twelve sober men
along a table, all staring straight at you;
twelve bearded heads, each on a goffered ruff
like boars' heads set on plates. All colour
is in the richly patterned crimson cloth
as though their blood had soaked down to enrich it.

The black-clad men look drained, deep lines
around their eyes and brows. You can't interpret
that gaze of weary triumph, maybe of something
momentous, until you read the label on the wall.
Across the battlefield of this sumptuous cloth
after hours of advances, retreats and compromise,
the diplomats of Spain and England have ended
twenty years of war on land and sea.

Corsica II, about 1959

After Alistair Grant

Here where trains sear the peace, only
sheep bells jangled on the slopes. Bees
seemed to drowse in heavy-scented flowers,

oil and grape juice trickled from the press.
Fierce men chafed at the foreign rule
and from Ajaccio Napoleon Bonaparte

rose up and caused a seismic shift in Europe.
Millions of years ago a granite backbone
thrust upwards from the sea and now these sweeping

brushmarks clothe its spurs with the glowing pink
of sunstroke, hours of blinding glare; vivid
slopes cascade to the plain where clumps

of heavy-headed trees, blue-green, are remnants
of the island forest – cork, holm oak, palms.

Czech Conscript

1942

He woke to the scratch of brushwood and a shower
of skylark song falling as the bird spiralled higher.
The scarecrow's coat had kept him dry in the hollow,
concealed his German uniform. Surely the song
was a good omen for slipping into France tonight,
that the Maquis would help him to England.

1985

In his breaks from grinding rocks in Sedimentology,
burnishing their colours, revealing trilobites, fossil ferns,
he takes up his violin, plays Bach or Bartok. The notes
spill out into the corridor, disperse into slanting sun.
Meaning music, I ask what he most enjoys.
He answers *Peace. Simply to live at peace.*

San Gimignano

Best was early morning when the church bells pealed,
harsh Tuscan voices shouted yard to yard, we had
melon, grapes, peaches, coffee on our terrace
with its roofscape of ridge tiles, spires and towers.
We'd walk across empty piazzas, alleyways still cool,
the towers asleep. By high stone buildings; severe,
small-windowed, we might almost meet their ghosts.

Colour was indoors – on the Duomo's Roman arches,
blue and white striped, its star-specked cobalt vault,
its frescos. As we emerged, mid-morning, heat thumped us
from above, rebounded from the steps. The town hummed,
people swarmed round gift shops, cafés, queued for
the tower or gelateria. Old men sat on plastic chairs,
still and inscrutable as the lizards sunning on town walls.

In Tuscany

Relentless sun bored down and we, mad dogs, walked out past walls
where lizards baked like cakes, through vineyards stripped of fruit,
along a dusty road across a plateau grey-brown with drought. Heat
hazed distance, bounced from the track, coursed sweat into my eyes.

A small church beckoned. We found it locked, but pushed open a door
in the high presbytery wall; stepped into a shock of cool green shade.
Water trickled from a basin, palms and ferns spread arching leaves
around a colonnade of slender pillars. We longed to rest, to cool,
bathe our feet, but knew ourselves intruders, closed the door and left.

Car Park

We stepped into exhaust fumes and M1 traffic grind
at Leicester Forest Services. Battled through ranks
of a jeans and T-shirt army marching to Costa and KFC

to pass an eager-faced young Indian, scarlet tunic
embroidered with glass beads and silver swirls,
two lovely girls, gorgeous in green and gold
encrusted with gold thread, emerald scarab wings.

Behind our car older ladies adjusted make-up and saris
and among a group of young bloods one stood out –
a maharajah surely, with his proud stance, jewelled kurta,
Parsi cap and pointed shoes. Against tarmac and cars

their Eastern colours blazed. Enhanced with kohl,
dark liquid eyes were those of princes, maharanis; until,
the marriage solemnised, their heavy garments would be
folded in tissue, sealed into boxes, returned to the hire firm.

At Pembroke Castle

Clowns send streams of bubbles
glinting in the sun
across the Inner Bailey.
Under his bowler hat
one has long dreadlocks,
another spins a hula hoop
while children stilt-walk.

We marvel at the Great Hall,
clump down a spiral staircase
to a large dark cavern,
Wogan's Cave. Eyes adjust
to its womb shape, opening
to the riverside, its puddled
hard-packed sandy floor.

Here naked children played
to the sounds of flint-knocks
as a man made tools, crackling
of a fire as smoke drifted.
Perhaps a thong held back
unruly hair and fire made
giants of them on the walls

Rackham

You turn the pages
become the child below
oaks or willows –
gnarled old men or crones
with faces kind or cruel
boughs reaching for you.

You hurry past
giants and goblins
with long sharp noses
long shrunk shanks
long knobbly feet
and fingers – to finger you.

You linger over dragonflies
hexed into fairies, but
greed and spite grafted
to the heads of birds and beasts
tip the story book back
into nightmare to haunt you.

The Thing

Once talk wove around Kelmscott's apple trees,
children scared birds from the strawberry bed.
Quiet came like frost. We do not speak of It,
except to closest friends. No others come.

The Thing first struck when Jenny was thirteen
and with that groan, the stiffening, dead eyes
and dragging breath she seemed to sink
into some deep and sunless tarn; unreachable.

Each time it is a dagger-thrust to me,
a punishment for guilt. The years and bromide
make her fat and slow. She seldom smiles,
no longer tries to jump from windows but

is always, always here. May bows her head
over embroidery. She will not marry now.
William's eyes are on his brush, caressing
willow leaves. He will not hear of an asylum.

Our Gang

Down behind the milk depot we would gather –
Wayne our leader brought out his matches, lit fags
stolen from his father the village bobby
passed them around us.

We would suck them nervously, puff the smoke out
trying not to cough or to gag or splutter.
Then we'd choose a street where the lights were beaming
curtains not drawn yet.

Quietly we'd inch along, stare in front rooms,
watch the Fosters eating their stew and dumplings.
Sam had told us how she had seen Miss Andrews
kissing the doctor.

Amy Thompson's bungalow was well lighted –
boys expected thrilling sights in her bedroom.
Girls all turned back, Wayne tried the gate, then panicked,
ran from the pit-bull.

Speech Training

We'd all recite *The rain in Spain*,
How now brown cow, *Peter Piper picked*,
or the finger pointed and you had to

stand and speak for 2 minutes about
carpets, knitting or the dining room.
My waffle floundered into silence.

She'd praise the girls who could project
the voice to resonate in their bony vaults.
Mine groped in the cellars of my throat.

In the last class when we could choose
I read Blunden's *The Pike* and she was
almost as amazed as the miller *at the whirl
in the water* when the pike emerged.

Severing

The slightest breeze will lift small seeds, each
with a downy parachute, from dandelion clocks.
Shepherd's purses split in two to loose their coin,
puffballs explode their spores like smoke.

Trees cut off the food supply, harden to a crust
and autumn winds supply the coup de grâce –
send drifts of leaves along the street, apples
dropping with soft thuds, ash keys spiralling.

But as I watch your Boeing taxi down
and feel my stomach tighten for the surge
of engine power, the tilt, the lift and climb
towards the clouds, I know we never stinted
food or love or threw you out or cut you off.
Unlike a tree I have not grown a scab.

Warming

Ice floes are cracking from the Arctic shore;
through kelp and plankton toxins filter down.
Saws grind and trees plunge to the forest floor.

Drag-nets break coral groves as men ignore
the laws, enmeshing porpoises which drown;
ice floes are cracking from the Arctic shore.

Our rivers flood more often than before
and hot dry summers turn our green lawns brown.
Saws grind and trees plunge to the forest floor.

On road and motorways there's more and more
traffic, and gridlock shackles every town.
Ice floes are cracking from the Arctic shore.

As smoke and fumes gush out, we can't ignore
our children gasping, bird flocks dwindling down;
saws grind and trees plunge to the forest floor.

Are humans fated, like the dinosaur,
to face extinction in a vast meltdown?
Ice floes are cracking from the Arctic shore.
Saws grind and trees plunge to the forest floor.

The Dragon Lands

As though a large hand shoves you on
or there's no stepping from a moving belt,
no rescue for your skiff swept on downstream
no anchor, trailing branch to grab.

Inside you are still twenty three, but know
how old your mother seemed at your age now –
how frail, incapable, in need of help,
more sleep, more medication.

Today your children do the cosseting,
in one way warming, though at times it seems
they really want to claim the middle ground
while you are eased out to the dragon lands.

Among the dragons – loss of stamina, good health
and dear ones. You can only fight.

Fading

We didn't worry until those shopping trips
when he came home empty-handed, shamefaced,
or he wandered the house, shoe brush in hand
forgetting what it was, or where he'd left the shoes.
When he washed up, the goulash dish went first
and glasses bobbed in grease and paprika.

Day Centre visits to give my mother respite
ended with a police hunt when he walked out –
so to a hospital where nurses called him George,
a male patient blacked his eye, a female
stalked him. On my last visit he sat silent,
eyes focused on some other place.

Ever After

On a grassy slope beside the church
the gravestone of Joseph Bell casts
a long shadow in the evening sun.

Outstretched arm, it just touches the grave
of *Alice, Loving Wife of Walter Penrose*,
as though even in death he reaches

out to her he loved, who loved him
in return, her husband not at all.

Meeting her Eyes

After waves of pain were dulled
by gas and air, the sharper stabs
were not, after rubber gloves
slipped on blood and mucus,
tearing my skin, after nine
lumbering months – I saw her.

I expected eyes unfocused
not that gaze, blue-violet –
the shock of it ran through me.
She too was curious, glad.
Almost a recognition.

Papier Blanc

It is a night over the Baltic. My cruise ship
purrs across its quiet pond. Programmed
for darkness, I stare at luminous sky.

It is a bedsheet, clean and starched,
stretched on a mattress, waiting to be creased
or torn or stained with piss, blood, semen.

It is the blindness of a blizzard in New York
which hurries all to shelter, fetters taxis, cars;
pinions synapses, deep-freezes my thoughts.

It is that moment when you've had the sedative,
been wheeled along a corridor, through rubber doors
to men in masks who prick your hand, ask you to count

and now I'm counting minutes since I first
stared at this white desert. Do I dare become
a tribe of ants to set out tracks just visible from space?

OS Sheet 189: Land's End

In the quiet concentration of the Drawing Section
I have spent months draughting coastline, contours,
roads and railway, cables, streams and rivers.
I've dashed in footpaths, boundaries, chevroned
gradients, marked bridges, embankments, cuttings.

Next I ink in the churches – round with a cross
in Penzance, square for Gulval and St Buryan.
Lighthouses at Newlyn and St Ives must have five rays.
Up to the moors for standing stones, tumuli; down for
trees in woods and parkland, tufts in the marshes.

Contour lines run close around the coast, and here
I dot in sand and shingle, outline rocks and cliffs;
lastly add names like Sinke Dean, Zawn Kellys,
Armed Knight. When it's done I stroke the whorls
of the contours with the whorls of my fingertips.

Pulse

The batter of rain on my umbrella,
gush of it along the gutter, dancing litter
above the drains. Growl of the bus I missed,

stink of the fumes it left. Drifts of daffodils
hanging their heads, the lane where I found
my rhythm. It swung me along, my steps

a metronome, showed me gravel washed clean
by rivulets, the smell of soaked grass and earth.
An approaching car made me shun the puddles,

but I had sticky buds to touch, spiders' webs
balancing raindrops, a wet old horse to talk to.

From the Kitchen Sink

I see white lights of snowdrops
against the dark, then daffodils
flying their yellow in March wind,
purple fires of crocus burning
under the hedge. Our blackbirds
stab the lawn, drag on elastic worms,
swirled-humbug snails are clamped
behind the clematis, a wolf spider
crouches on its web, legs braced
for messages along the threads.
Fruit trees hunch their knotted limbs,
bark contoured by the sun. In buds
bridal-white blossom, leafy shade,
a thrush's nest, the luscious plums
are tightly furled. Already raspberries
are testing the air with ragged green.

Wasps

As with ton-up boys
   the first thing was
      a hostile hum
         the faintest trace
      then louder louder
   as the tiger-insect neared,
a black and yellow
menace. At tea
   under the apple tree
      it would hover, land
         on the lip of your cup
      circle a head; freeze
   the cool ones, panic
the hot, who'd flap
spill tea or run.
      Gangs raided jampots
     at that tea garden
        by the river, jewelled
     your scone with threat.
   Where have they gone?
No more bicarb
on stings, dead bodies
   on the window-sills,
      no drunkards on windfall apples,
        pot-holes in the plums,
     no flight path
   under the soffit
papery nests in the loft.

In 2014 wasps seemed to have disappeared

Thread

They moved in
many years ago
pervade my house
and cannot be
exterminated,
hang in corners
by a single thread
upside down
like a jellyfish
trailing intestines
but are beautiful
in their way
small bodied
long thin legs
so they move
like giraffes
or stilt-walkers.
On a stepladder
I lift a jamjar
below them, clap
a card on top
carry out the
dark corner
dry dust lovers
to drop them
on moist grass
or sun-flecked leaf
but always find
another tiptoeing
across the ceiling,
sleeping like a climber
bivouacked on rock-face,
dangling from that
anchoring thread
finer than a hair
strong as a hawser.

Gown

Displayed at the Royal Shakespeare Theatre

The skirt's slim black net tatter will mist the legs;
its bodice is made up of evening gloves, off-white
and shades of grey. Like living creatures
they snake and intertwine, the fingers
pointing upwards in appeal or search.
Nothing to say whether Peaseblossom, Cobweb,
Mustardseed or Moth wore this. My money's
on Cobweb for the cloudy greys, the way
they will insinuate each crack and corner,
befog our minds and mystify our dreams.

Master Glover

Ladies' kidskin gloves, satin-soft, with slender fingers
hang behind lozenges of bleary window glass
with gentlemen's doeskin gauntlets, intricately worked,
purses and pouches of buckskin, coney fur muffs.

Deer, sheep and goat pelts musk the workroom
with lambskin and kidskin fluid as water. Outside,
the stink of lime and tanning pits. Inside, the rub
of hides drawn over and over a staking beam

to soften them for the whittawer and master glover,
Master Shakspere. He smooths and cuts a skin
watched by a bright-eyed boy he hopes one day
will shape and stitch up even finer wares.

Barbers' Bowl
Ashmolean Museum

I peer through glass at a rare survivor;
1740s porcelain. Sturdy, in blue and white,
the wide rim has a bite out, a hollow for soap.
Tendrils, flowers and leaves scroll round,
cherubs flaunt themselves beside a fleur-de-lys
and in the bowl, houses with tiled roofs crowd,
one with a cart entrance, trees behind. Surely
no surgeon-barber pulling teeth behind his pole
had such an article. In some great house
lackeys must have draped milord in white,
held the arced cut-out close against his neck,
steadied the water. A badger-hair brush,
vigorously lathered, would foam his whiskers
into meringue, drop cloudlets over fleur-de-lys,
putti, tendrils, leaves and flowers. Scummed
milky water would drown the small town.

The Potato Eaters
Vincent van Gogh

They seem to be underground.
Only an oil lamp's feeble glow
lights this family at the table.

The mother's white-capped head is bowed,
weariness brands both parents' faces;
the patient resignation of draught oxen.

A warm drink in her knobbly fingers,
the grandmother looks contented.
The boy is alert and focused on the food,

his sister apprehensive, fearing her father's
reproof when she scoops another nugget,
but he seems comatose. A life bent double

in the fields, a diet of potatoes, has grown
their lumpy noses, flabby lips, rough skin;
has turned them, year by year, into potatoes.

Disciples

Stanley Spencer: The Last Supper, 1920

They are fishtails in a box
rowers heaving the boat along

sea birds perched on the gunwale
quietly waiting on His word.

Waves swell beneath the table's deck
Christ at the helm divines his course

John leans to see the hand of God
break bread to cast on the waters.

Hilda, Unity and Dolls
Stanley Spencer 1937

Lips are the things you notice first –
the humans' full and sensual like his,
dolls' in the rigor of a rosebud smirk.

Next necks – Unity's frail as a mushroom's,
dolls' drainpipe hard. Hilda's rope-like tendons
groan with the stress that's echoed in the set
of her mouth, her inward-looking eyes.

One eye is severed by her spectacles' steel rim,
edge of the picture has trepanned her heavy hair
as though he knew, not knowing, that her apathy
came not from cussedness but illness.

The child whose name had now a bitter taste
stares out, touch of defiance in her lifted chin,
her eyes clear windows. Boredom looks out,
perhaps suppressed dislike, a sense of wrong.

As for the dolls, their masks with black-hole eyes
are sinister, grotesque. Only my fancy, surely,
that their names might be Dorothy and Patricia.

Loch Alsh

This finger the sea dips into land
is blown to wavelets by the wind
over pens of leaping salmon.
Clouds dawdle over Eilean Donan,
shawl the Five Sisters.

We hope for sea otters, sometimes
spot a V-shaped wake, but always
that of a seal. Along the shore
herons are spaced out, each one poised
to pounce into wavering water.

Emerging from conifers into light
we find a ruined broch, half the height
it was. The massive curving walls
of stone gave clansmen vantage
to scan the loch for invading ships.

The shock of my first golden eagle
glimpsed for a moment high on a pine.
Sensing its alien world of hunt and kill,
mountain crags, glides and deadly drops,
its ancient right to lordship of this place.

Greater Spotted

The woodpecker's a hammerhead, you hear
it knocking in the distance in the woods
and a dead branch of our old damson tree's
been tunnelled through just like a Henry Moore.

They often scare the smaller birds away
when clinging to the feeder's bottom rung
their feet with two claws forward, two claws back,
head through the bars to jab the hazelnuts.

Their livery of black and white and red
stands out. The other day one fastened on
the entrance to the blue tits' nesting box
and pecking to enlarge the hole rapped out,
resounding like a drum, fortissimo –
a paean to his house building and hope.

Ghostly

On winter evenings when the dark wraps round
we switch on lights and pull the curtains tight.
We're safe here with the boiler's soothing sound,
forget the world outside where creatures fight
for life, for food and space to rear their young.
Out there the slinking fox scents every clue –
a pheasant's passage, trace of muntjac dung
between moon-silvered graves and brooding yew.
And from this world I hear a ghostly cry
in folklore said to prophesy a death –
the tawny owl which silently and high
glides through the frosted trees and with each breath
sends out that wavering call to find his mate
and scans the ground where voles must chance their fate.

Mine

We'd always waited in Arrivals –
noisy with voices, the Tannoy,
rumble of suitcase wheels.
Aidan watched the screen for his plane,
Emily wriggled in my arms
as he came striding out.

This time they said don't come
to the airport, he'll be sedated.
Come to the hospital. So I'm here alone
grasping the rail of a stomach-sinking lift,
walking the corridor smelling floor polish
and the foam on my fingers. Ward 5
and I see him at once, his bedclothes
over a frame. I clutch my bag of fruit,
step towards his years of physio,
prosthetic legs, learning to walk
between bars, with sticks, without.

Our Dream

We knew, of course, the journey would be long
and dangerous, my mother old and frail,
the children trusting, so that it seemed wrong

to put their lives at risk when we set sail
in this old overloaded rubber boat
which took on water, forcing us to bale

with just one plastic pail to stay afloat.
The wind was rising, no stars in the sky
to guide us on to Lesbos, so remote

and as we huddled close the waves grew high
crashed down and flipped us over with a swirl,
flung many to the depths and some to die –

for here we lost our precious baby girl.
But strong arms pulled me, mother, son and wife
to safety – shaking, grieving for our pearl.

So now we're in a camp, a dreary life,
long queues for food, not knowing when we'll leave,
my mother sick, for cholera is rife –

but still we have our dream, we still believe.

After Sonnet 64, Shakespeare

When I have seen how we have poisoned seas
with micro-plastic never to decay;
scarred landscapes, nuclear waste, the death of trees,
how hives collapse, song thrushes fall away.

When I have seen tall ice-cliffs fracture, fall,
watched people wading down a flooded street;
when maize crops shrivelled by the drought appal,
raise ribs, leave infants suckling a dry teat;

Then, Shakespeare, does your balance overturn
for Nature cannot heal the spoils of men.
The wise set targets, try to halt the harm
but tides of appetite grow strong again.

Though you beyond your mistress had no fears
We tremble for our children down the years.

Swift

Prepared skin at Reading Museum

A shock to see you
lying here

no life, wings tight –
a feathered bullet

which rode the currents
skated in the sky

whose high-pitched cries
pierced space

Two Rivers Press has been publishing in and about Reading since 1994. Founded by the artist Peter Hay (1951–2003), the press continues to delight readers, local and further afield, with its varied list of individually designed, thought-provoking books.

The poems in this collection are set in Janson – a lively modern revival of a traditional serif typeface with high stroke contrast and a large x-height to aid legibility. For the headings, we've used Parisine, a contemporary sanserif, to provide a counterpoint to the classic feel of Janson, and to distinguish notes and epigraphs from the poems.